TRANSLATIONS
OF THE CHINESE CHARACTERS
ON THE BACK COVER:

老子 LAO TZU   道德經 TAO TE CHING   德 DE (virtue)   美 MI (beauty)

Three Chinese characters make up Demi's chop, or signature:

DE
MI — 德美知 — HO

Demi's name and her chop translate to
"One Who Celebrates Beauty and Virtue."

Margaret K. McElderry Books An imprint of Simon & Schuster Children's Publishing Division
1230 Avenue of the Americas, New York, New York 10020 Copyright © 2007 by Demi All rights
reserved, including the right of reproduction in whole or in part in any form. Book design by
Michael Nelson The text for this book is set in Hiroshige. The illustrations for this book are
rendered in paint and ink. Title calligraphy by Jeanyee Wong Manufactured in China
2 4 6 8 10 9 7 5 3 1
LIBRARY OF CONGRESS CATALOGING-IN-PUBLICATION DATA:
Demi. The legend of Lao Tzu and the Tao Te Ching / Demi.—1st ed. p. cm.
ISBN-13: 978-1-4169-1206-4   ISBN-10: 1-4169-1206-1
1. Laozi. 2. Laozi. Dao de jing. I. Title. BL1930.D46 2007
299.5'1482—dc22   2005029695

FIRST
EDITION

The Legend of Lao Tzu and the Tao Te Ching

DEMI

MARGARET K. McELDERRY BOOKS   NEW YORK LONDON TORONTO SYDNEY

THIS IS THE LEGEND OF LAO TZU,
who may or may not have been born;
who may or may not have founded Taoism,
one of the greatest religions in the world . . .

. . . and who may or may not have written
one of the greatest books of wisdom in the world:
the Tao Te Ching, or the "Way of Heaven."

Some say that on the fourteenth of September, 604 B.C., in the village of Ch'u Jen, in the country of K'u, in the kingdom of Ch'u in ancient China, Lao Tzu was born, and nine heavenly dragons flew down from Heaven to wash his body. Lao Tzu's mother had carried him for eighty-one years, and so at birth he already had snow-white hair and large ears, and could walk.

His name meant "Old Wise One," and he was said to be the Spirit of the Highest Venerable Lord of Eternal Tao, who could harness the clouds' energies, walk on the essence of the sun, and fly with the stars. Lao Tzu was born wise, and already knew the magic arts of energy, medicine, healing, longevity, clairvoyance, protection, and transcendence. He could also talk to animals.

Once Lao Tzu was asked how he found the Way of Heaven, and he said, "I made a great effort: I tried and tried and tried to find it, but I couldn't. Then one day as I was sitting under a tree, a dry leaf fell, slowly moving with the wind. The wind moved north; the leaf moved north; the wind moved south; the leaf moved south; then the wind stopped—and the leaf fell down and rested beautifully on the earth. Then again there was some wind, and again the leaf rose high in the sky.

"Suddenly I became that dry leaf; and suddenly I understood the Way of Heaven. No longer was I separate from Heaven, but I was a part of Heaven. Wherever Heaven went, I went.

"If it changed its mind,
I changed my mind.
If it stopped, I stopped.
If it flowed, I flowed.
And that is how I found the Way."

Once Lao Tzu was traveling on his donkey when a messenger from the Emperor came up to him and said, "The Emperor has heard about your great wisdom and wants you to be a part of his court." Lao Tzu was very polite but declined. When the messenger was gone, Lao Tzu began to furiously wash his ears with water, and then he washed his donkey's ears too.

Someone asked the Old Wise One what in the world he was doing, and Lao Tzu replied, "I wash my ears because even one political word is dangerous. I wash my donkey's ears because donkeys are very political.

"Knowing the messenger was from the Emperor, the donkey immediately became proud and already is walking with a new strut. Being a donkey, he understands the language of the court, which is full of donkeys."

Eventually Lao Tzu did become palace secretary in the Chinese imperial capital at Loyang, and then astrologer and keeper of the archives for the Court of Chou.

Some consider Lao Tzu the greatest teacher of all time. He had many disciples, whom he taught Heaven's way by example and silent meditation. He said, "The truth that can be told is not the real truth; the truth that can be told becomes untrue immediately."

At 160 years of age, Lao Tzu had seen enough corruption and decline in the Court of Chou to make him want to leave and live his virtuous life in peace elsewhere. Riding northwest in a chariot drawn by a dark-blue ox, he arrived at the Han Ku Pass. The guard at the pass was Yin Hsi, one of his own disciples. He said to Lao Tzu, "Unless you write a book for the good of all mankind, I am not going to let you pass. This is the debt you have to pay to all the world."

And so for three days Lao Tzu sat at the Han Ku Pass and wrote the Tao Te Ching, one of the greatest books of all time.

Lao Tzu gave the Tao Te Ching to Yin Hsi to help
humanity live according to the Way of Heaven.
Then Lao Tzu departed.

Yin Hsi immediately began spreading the Tao Te Ching throughout China.

The Tao Te Ching has five thousand Chinese characters. It has two sections, one that tells of the Way of Heaven (Tao) and the other that tells of its virtue (Te). Here are twenty of the eighty-one verses.

THE ENERGY OF THE UNIVERSE

The Way of Heaven is like a well
that is used but never used up.
It is eternal, and the creator
of everything in the world.
In it all sharpness is dulled,
all tangles untied,
all glare shut out,
all dust swept away.
Where did it come from?
I do not know.
It is older than eternity.

THE VERY BEST

The very best are like water:
They benefit all things without trying to;
they are content with low places that others dislike.
That is why water is so near to Heaven's Way.
The very best in their homes love simplicity,
in their hearts love what is deep,
in their words love what is true,
in friendship love what is gentle.
The very best in their world love what is peaceful,
in government love what is orderly,
in deeds love what is right,
in actions love what is timely.

It is because they do not compete
with others that they are loved by all.

SILENCE

Those who know don't speak.
Those who speak don't know.
Close your mouth,
dull your senses,
smooth what's sharp,
untie all tangles,
shut out all glare,
wipe away all dust.
This is your real Self.
Be on Heaven's Way
without desires or dislikes,
benefit or harm,
honor or disgrace. This is
being Heaven's highest,
for one under Heaven.

KNOWING

Without leaving his door
the Wise One knows everything under Heaven.
Without looking out his window
he knows the Way of Heaven.
For the farther one travels,
the less one knows.
Therefore the Wise One arrives without going,
sees Heaven without looking,
does nothing,
yet achieves everything.

JUST BE ORDINARY

It is because people say some things are beautiful
that the idea of ugliness exists.
It is because people say some things are good
that the idea of evil exists.

Being and non-being come out of each other.
Difficult and easy are part of each other.
Long and short define each other;
high and low determine each other;
sharp and flat harmonize each other;
front and back follow each other.

Therefore the Wise One
acts without doing,
shows without saying,
accepts without reservation,
receives but doesn't possess,
raises but doesn't own,
guides but doesn't depend,
succeeds but isn't proud.
And for this very reason
he is successful.

BEING STILL

The dark is the root of the light.
The still is the source of all motion.
Though the Wise One travels all day,
he never leaves his heart.
However beautiful the view,
he stays serenely quiet.
How foolish is a great lord
who runs around like a fool,
losing himself to all the world,
and the chance of Heaven.

MODERATION

Stretch a bow to the very full,
and you'll wish you'd stopped in time.
Grind a sword to its sharpest edge,
and you'll find it soon grows dull.
When gold and jade fill your house,
you'll find they can't be safely guarded.

Wealth and fame bring pride,
which brings ruin in its train.
When your work is done, then stop.
Such is Heaven's Way.

WINNERS

The best charioteers don't rush ahead.
The best fighters don't show their strength.
The greatest leaders win without a fight.
The richest salesmen act with great humility.
This is the power that comes with not fighting.
This is the Way that Heaven uses people.
And this is the way to win.

PUSHING

He who stands on tiptoe isn't steady.
He who pushes ahead doesn't go far.
He who tries to be a star clouds his own way.
He who defines himself cannot be distinct.
He who boasts of what he'll do cannot succeed.
He who's proud of his own work creates nothing that will last.
This is like feeding people
who are already full.
They will be rejected
by Heaven and its Way.

BALANCE

If you try to change the world,
you won't succeed.
For the world is like a holy vessel,
dangerous to toy with.
Those who mess with it harm it.
Those who grab at it lose it.
For in the world some are first and some are last;
some are loud and some are quiet;
some are quick and some are slow;
some are winners and some are losers.
Therefore the Wise One accepts things as they are,
rejects all extremes,
and balances right in the middle.

THE WORLD

The five colors confuse the eye.
The five sounds deafen the ear.
The five flavors spoil the taste.
The five thoughts confuse the mind.
The five wishes weaken the heart.
Therefore the Wise One trusts his heart
above the world,
lets all things come and go,
and focuses on Heaven.

EMPTY SPACE

Thirty spokes put together make a wheel,
but it's in the space where there is nothing
that the usefulness of the wheel depends.
Clay that's shaped will make a pot,
but it's in the space where there is nothing
that the usefulness of the pot depends.
Wood that's cut will make a house,
but it's in the space where there is nothing
that the usefulness of the house depends.
Therefore we should value not only what is,
but also what is not.

ILLUSION

When a wise man hears the Tao,
he immediately starts to practice it.
When an average man hears the Tao,
he doesn't know whether he believes it or not.
When a foolish man hears the Tao,
he laughs out loud,
and if he didn't laugh out loud,
it wouldn't be worth the name of Tao.

It is said: The way to the light seems to be dark;
the way forward seems to go backward.
The way that is straight seems to be curved.
True power seems to be weak.
True purity seems impure.
True stability seems unstable.
True naturalness seems to be fake.
The greatest art seems to be simple.
The greatest love seems to be small.
The greatest wisdom seems to be silly.

The Way of Heaven is invisible,
yet it can be seen.
It creates and completes everything.

SEEMINGLY SO

What is most perfect seems imperfect;
yet it is complete.
What is most full seems empty,
yet it can be emptied forever.
What is most straight seems crooked;
what is great art seems artless;
what is great wisdom seems foolish.

Movement overcomes cold;
and staying still overcomes heat.
The Wise One by his serene calm
lets Heaven move in him.

KNOW YOURSELF

To know others is intelligence;
to know yourself is wisdom.
To conquer others is power;
to conquer yourself is strength.
To be content with yourself
is to be rich.
To be discontent with yourself
is to be poor.
Keep the essence of Heaven inside yourself,
and you will never die.

KNOWING

To know when you don't know is wise.
To think you know when you don't know is not.
Only when you see sickness as sickness can you become well.
The Wise One's way of curing sickness
is to make people see what is what,
and thus be completely cured.

GENTLE

What is the gentlest of all
overcomes the hardest of all.
Without substance
the Way of Heaven enters where there is no space.
Non-action wins over action.
But to know there can be teaching without words,
action without action,
few can understand.

HEAVEN'S WAY

He whose braveness lies in war, kills.
He whose braveness lies in peace, gives life.
Either can win or lose,
but Heaven hates what it hates.
No one can know the reason why.
Heaven's Way is not to fight and yet to conquer,
not to speak and yet to be answered,
not to call, yet things come by themselves.
Heaven's Way is quiet, invisible, and planned.
Heaven's net is wide, yet nothing slips through.

GOVERNING

Governing a large country
is like cooking a small fish.
It can be spoiled with too much poking.
Center the country in Heaven's Way,
and evil cannot enter.
Not that it won't try to;
but you can move out of its way.
When evil has nothing to oppose,
it will disappear by itself.

TRUE WORDS

True words are not fine sounding.
Fine-sounding words are not true.
A good man doesn't prove by arguing,
and he who argues isn't good.
True wisdom comes not from much learning.
Much learning means little wisdom.
The Wise One has few things,
but he gives them away,
and look! He has more than before.
When the last has been given away,
look! He has even more than before!
For Heaven's Way
is to shape without force,
and the Wise One's way
is to act without trying.

Lao Tzu traveled through the Han Ku Pass.
Then, some say, he traveled through the floating sands of Central Asia.

Some say he traveled through the drifting snows of high Tibet,
giving the Law of Heaven along the way.

Some say Lao Tzu ascended on a beautiful white stork to the Taoist Heaven called Shou Shan. There he met the Taoist Immortals—and the Heavenly Empress of the West, who held the peach of immortality for him.

On the path to Eternity, Lao Tzu was blessed by the Three Star Gods of Longevity, Wealth, and Happiness, and finally by the Jade Emperor, ruler of all the Taoist Heavens.

Though given numerous exalted titles, Lao Tzu is remembered as the "Old Wise One" who taught the virtues of softness and yielding, of innocence and peace—great lessons for everyone, anytime, anywhere.

TAO

The Way of Heaven

I CHING

Book of Changes
about fortunes

T'AI CHI

The Harmony of Heaven; made up
of complementaries such as yin/yang,
dark/light, and female/male.

MIRRORS

Reflectors of Heaven

GEESE

Happiness

TAOIST

SYMBOLS

AND

THEIR

MEANINGS

**THE "OLD
WISE ONE"**

Lao Tzu

JADE EMPEROR

Ruler of the Taoist Heavens

DRAGON

Wealth; Wisdom; Power; East

PHOENIX

Wife of the Dragon;
Bird of the Heavenly Empress;
South; Red

THREE STAR GODS

CRANE

Longevity

SNAKE

Cunning; North

Shou Hsing: Long Life
Lu Hsing: Wealth and Power
Fu Hsing: Happiness

PINE TREES
Nobility

SWORD
Energy

TIGER
Power; West

DEER
Longevity; Good Fortune

TALISMAN
Protector

THREE TREASURES
Vitality; Energy; Spirit

TORTOISE
Longevity; North

FIVE COLORS
Azure; Red; Yellow; White; Black

HEAVENLY EMPRESS
Hsi Wang Mu;
Queen Mother of
the West;
Mother Goddess;
Ruler of Immortals

FIVE SOUNDS
Kung; Shang; Chiao; Chih; Yu

GUARDIAN
Ta Shih Yeh;
Protector from
Ghosts

FIVE FLAVORS
Sour; Bitter; Sweet; Acrid; Salty

FIVE WISHES
Wisdom; Joy; Compassion;
Generosity; Equality

FIVE THOUGHTS
Wisdom; Peace; Equality;
Compassion; Judgment

MUSHROOM (FUNGUS)
Longevity

STARS
Fortune

IMMORTALS
Angels of Heaven

PEACH
Longevity

FISH
Abundance

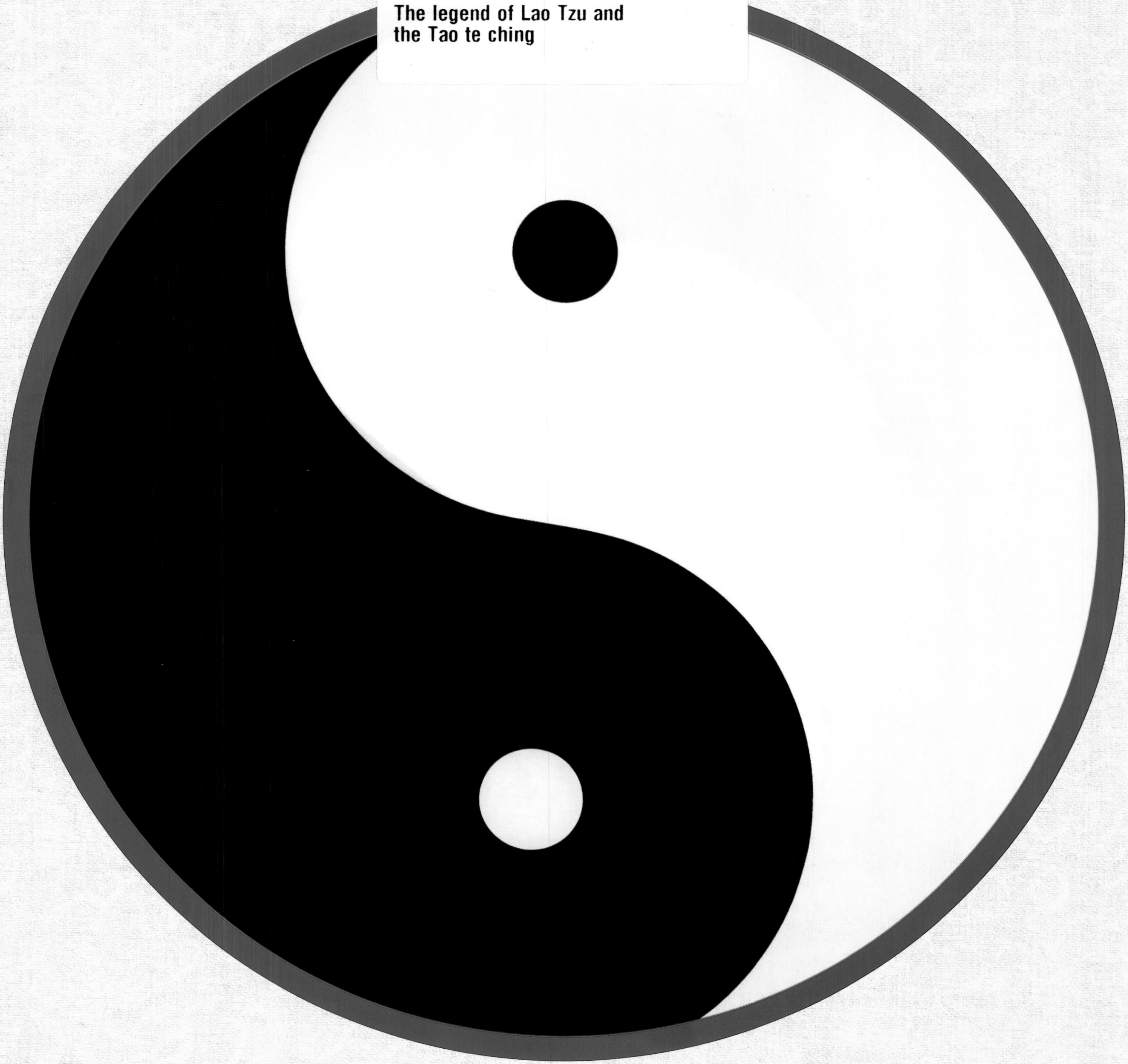